How to use this book

D1407226

Follow the advice, in italics, given for you on each page.
Support the children as they read the text that is shaded in cream.
Praise *the children at every step!*
Detailed guidance is provided in the Read Write Inc. Phonics Handbook.

---

9 reading activities

Children:

1 *Practise reading the speed sounds.*
2 *Read the green, red and challenge words for the non-fiction text.*
3 *Listen as you read the introduction.*
4 *Discuss the vocabulary check with you.*
5 *Read the non-fiction text.*
6 *Re-read the non-fiction text and discuss the 'questions to talk about'.*
7 *Re-read the non-fiction text with fluency and expression.*
8 *Answer the questions to 'read and answer'.*
9 *Practise reading the speed words.*

Speed sounds

Consonants *Say the pure sounds (do not add 'uh').*

f	l	m	n	r	s	v	z	sh	th	ng
ff	ll	mm	nn	rr	ss	ve	zz			nk
ph	le	mb	kn	wr	**(se)**		se			
					c		s			
					ce					

b	c	d	g	h	j	p	qu	t	w	x	y	ch
bb	k	dd	gg		j	pp		tt	**(wh)**			tch
	ck				ge							

Vowels *Say the vowel sound and then the word, eg 'a', 'at'.*

at	hen	in	on	up	day	see	high	blow
	head				make	tea	smile	home
						happy	lie	no
						he	find	

zoo	look	car	for	fair	whirl	shout	boy
brute			door	care	nurse	cow	spoil
blue			snore		letter		
			yawn				

*Each box contains one sound but sometimes more than one grapheme. Focus graphemes are **circled**.*

Green words

Read in Fred Talk (pure sounds).

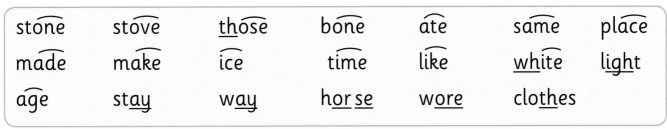

stone	stove	those	bone	ate	same	place
made	make	ice	time	like	white	light
age	stay	way	hor se	wore	clothes	

Read in syllables.

com` pu` ters → computers   mo` bile → mobile

ant` e` lope → antelope

Read the root word first and then with the ending.

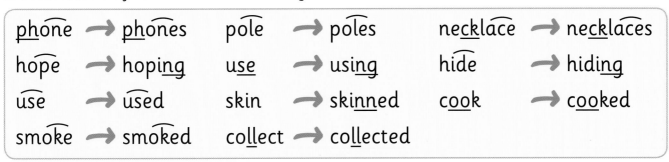

phone → phones   pole → poles   necklace → necklaces

hope → hoping   use → using   hide → hiding

use → used   skin → skinned   cook → cooked

smoke → smoked   collect → collected

Red words

of   some   the   there   they   to
was   were   what

Challenge words

because   bison   museums
caught   women   people

The Stone Age

Introduction

What do you know about the Stone Age? Did you know that it is a period in history, a very long time ago? In this book you will learn all about how Stone Age people lived and worked.

Written by Gill Munton

Vocabulary check

Discuss the meaning (as used in the non-fiction text) after the children have read the word.

	definition
Ice Age	*a period of time when snow and ice covered more of the Earth*
bison	*a large shaggy-haired ox*
antelope	*an animal like a deer*
skinned	*took the skin off*
stove	*a sort of oven*
smoked	*cooked in the smoke of a fire*
flint	*a very hard stone*
harpoon	*weapon with a sharp arrow-like point attached to the end*
museum	*a place that displays things from the past*

Punctuation to note:

Stone Age	*Capital letters for names*
?	*Question mark at the end of each question*
–	*To show a pause before more information follows*
birds' eggs	*Apostrophe to show who or what owns something (the eggs belong to the birds)*

Long, long ago, when the Ice Age was over, there was a time known as the Stone Age.

This is because the men used stone to make tools.

There were no farms, no shops, no TV, no mobile phones and no computers.

What did they eat?

People went hunting, hoping to see a horse, a bison or an antelope.

They killed the beast, skinned it and cut it up.

They cooked the meat on a sort of stove.

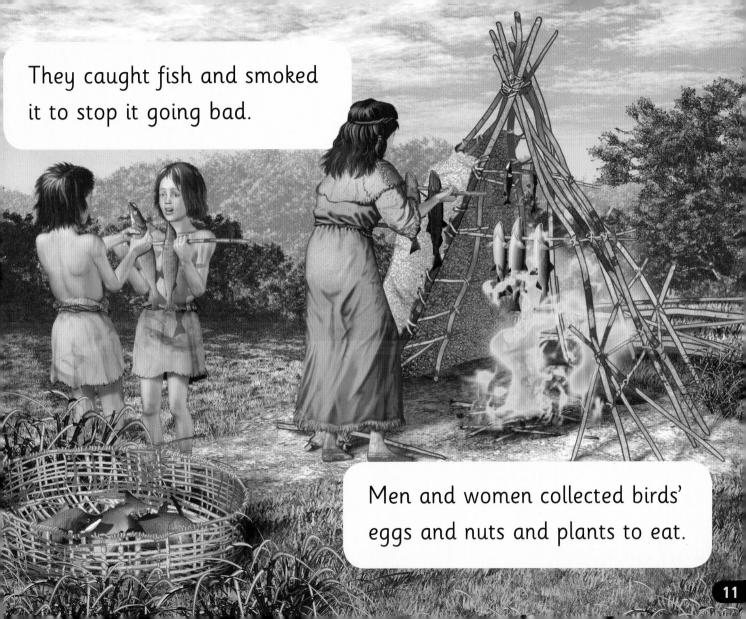

They caught fish and smoked it to stop it going bad.

Men and women collected birds' eggs and nuts and plants to eat.

What were the homes like?

Because people followed the animals to get meat, they didn't stay in the same place for long.

They made huts or tents, using poles made from branches and animal skins.

They slept in caves, too.

What were the clothes like?

People wore clothes made of animal skins.

If they were going hunting, they wore antelope horns as a way of hiding from the animals.

How did they make tools?

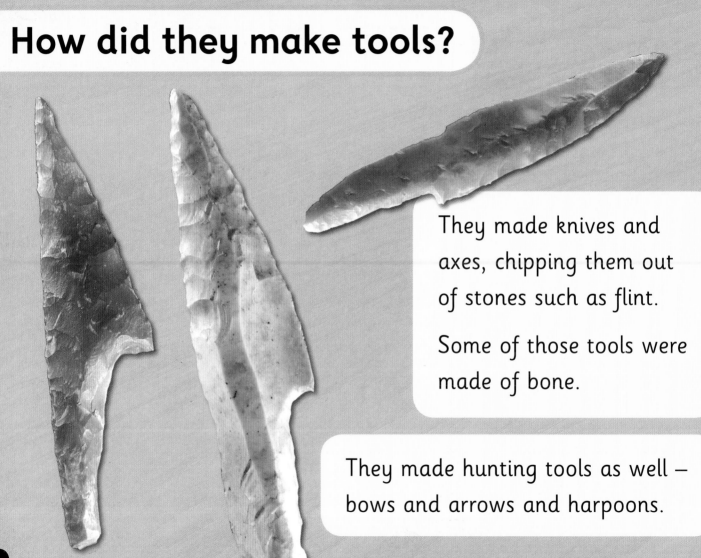

They made knives and axes, chipping them out of stones such as flint.

Some of those tools were made of bone.

They made hunting tools as well – bows and arrows and harpoons.

Were there Stone Age artists?

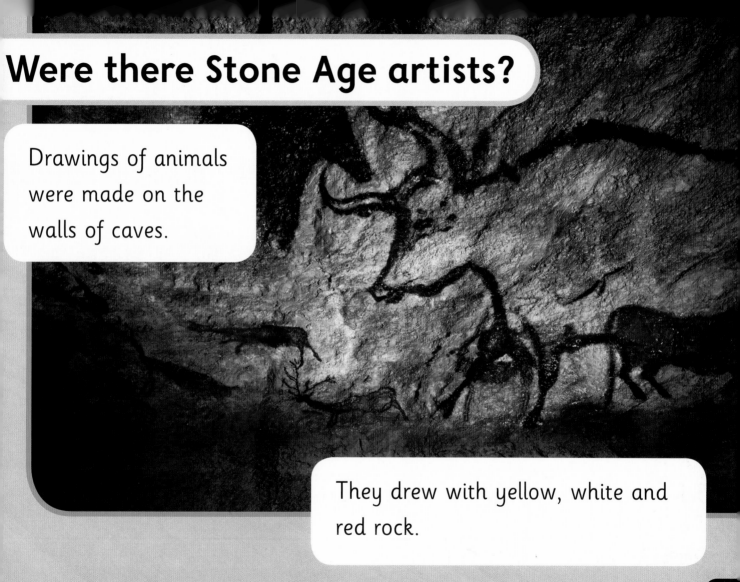

Drawings of animals were made on the walls of caves.

They drew with yellow, white and red rock.

They made carvings from bones and stone.

They made necklaces, rings and bracelets, using beads made from animals' teeth.

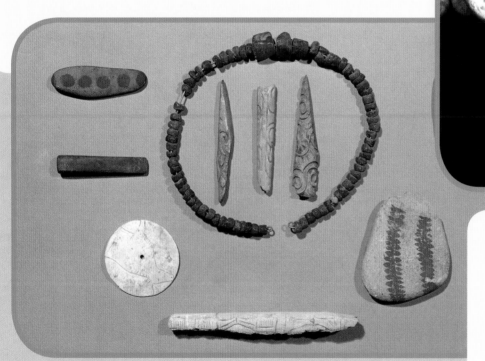

You can see some things made in the Stone Age in museums.

Questions to talk about

Re-read the page. Read the question to the children. Tell them whether it is a FIND IT *question or* PROVE IT *question.*

FIND IT	PROVE IT
✓ Turn to the page	✓ Turn to the page
✓ Read the question	✓ Read the question
✓ Find the answer	✓ Find your evidence
	✓ Explain why

Page 10:	PROVE IT	*Why did Stone Age people go hunting?*
Page 11:	FIND IT	*How did they stop fish going bad?*
Pages 10–11:	FIND IT	*What food did they eat?*
Page 12:	FIND IT	*Why didn't Stone Age people stay in the same place for very long?*
Page 15:	FIND IT	*What colours did Stone Age artists use?*
Page 16:	PROVE IT	*What sort of jewellery did they have in the Stone Age?*

Questions to read and answer

(Children complete without your help.)

1 What did Stone Age people use to make tools?
2 What were Stone Age homes made of?
3 What hunting tools did they make?
4 What did Stone Age artists draw?
5 What were animal teeth used for?